NEW H

MW01116337

LIVE FREE OR DIE

Co-written Laurel A Smith
Cory Smith & Dwight Smith

Illustrations by Michelle Banning

This Story is Dedicated to our Revolutionary War Relatives;

Scranton, Lang, Rand, & Sischo

And to any Lost Lives or Loved Ones in the Pursuit of Freedom.

Thank you to Ed Smith, husband, and father, for his insight and patience.

Also, to Pam LaFountain and Mike Wright for their editing and expertise.

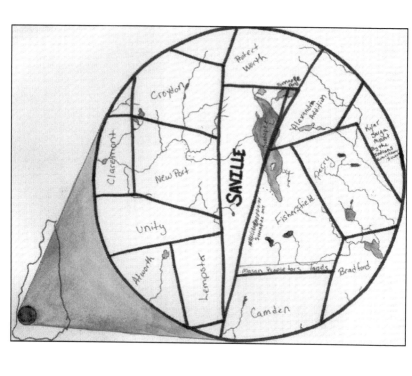

SAVILLE, NH

1768 - 1781

NEW HAMPSHIRE WARRIOR

LIVE FREE OR DIE

Table of Contents

"Look out. Here he comes!" old man Stephen walked through the door of The Stumble Inn Tavern.

William and George shuddered as a man sat down, groaning pulling his lame arm onto the bar counter and ordered a round and a meal. Stephen drank his beer, had a bite to eat, and stared straight ahead.

William whispered, "He never says a word."

"And he's a little off, ain't he?" George replied.

"Get the cards.

"What for?"

"We'll cut the deck. Low card clears the old man's plates."

"Aw, low card again." said William. He had been losing a lot at that game, lately. As William reached to grab the plate, the old man turned and looked right at him, eye to eye.

"Do you boys wanna hear a story?"

William froze. "Sure." William squeaked, his mouth trembling.

George cautiously leaned in to hear the man's words, but to make sure not to get too close.

Old Man Stephen began his tale, "During the war my friends and I would draw cards, just like you boys. But, for us low man would mean being in the front of the line."

George stammered, "Wha, wha, what line?"

"Why the fighting line." Stephen sputtered back, "not something as safe as taking an old man's dishes away."

The boys sheepishly looked at their feet, embarrassed that they had made such a big deal as to who would clean up after the old soldier.

"Did you ever get a low card?" George asked, surprised at his own courage. Old Man Stephen had always intimidated him.

"Aw sure, but luckily it just wasn't my time when I did." he comfortably replied.

William questioned, "Time for what?"

"Time to be with the Lord. You know, killed, boy."

"Oh yah, sorry."

"Don't be sorry. I'm not. I'm here, ain't I? I wasn't much older than you when I started my duty."

"Really?" George perked up.

"How old are you?" Stephen inquired.

"Thirteen and a half, sir." he replied proudly.

"Yup, almost two years older, I was fifteen when I began my service to The Sons of Liberty."

George pointed back and forth to William and himself, "We love those stories. Our families were on the same side as the Patriots."

William piped in, "We've also seen the Liberty Tree many times on our way to get grain a few towns over at the mill."

Stephen looked serious, "That wasn't an easy trip years ago. My great grandfather lived many miles from the mill. He did this one trip he was the only white settler in the town, of course his wife and kids were there. The only other person was a native settler whose family and tribe had moved on. The native settler was determined to live out his days there. Which he did peacefully." He continued, "It was winter and as I

4

just told ya, he had a wife, a five-year-old son, and a newborn. They had scarcely anything left to eat. He headed out to the mill, which was a two-day trip each way.

Stephen ordered another drink which the boys quickly got him. He took a long deep swallow and kept talking, "When he was halfway there a fierce snowstorm blew in. He was stuck at the mill for 5 days, with no way to get word back to his family. His wife was sure he was dead. She tended to the house and children as best she could, but she had her own battle to fight. Tragically, the infant died, and she had no food left to feed the five-year-old. Only her mother's milk to keep the small child alive. She was certain they would also both die."

William gasped, "Did they die?"

"Nope, she survived and so did the kid. She was a strong and courageous woman, keeping her sanity through that whole ordeal was tough!"

"Did the dad return?" George wanted to know.

"In time, and by that spring two more families had joined the settlement, one of which was actual family, and that helped ease the burden."

William looked at the Old Man, "It sounds like your family lived through some tough times back then."

6

Stephen nodded, "Those were my ancestors, didn't know them; that was just hearsay."

"Do you believe it?" William asked.

"Sure do, I say it's the truth. But I got some tales that I know are truth because, I lived them." he motioned to the boys, "Pull up a stool.

CHAPTER TWO: HIS STORY

"My family came to Seville from the coast. We had relatives that were captains and shipbuilders there. Some of them were even sailors that shipped dried fish to the West Indies. My granddad's family was in lumber and had ties with the mast trees being used by King George of England. We needed to move west to get more trees but the further west we traveled the harder it was to transport them back. "

"Why?" William asked.

Stephen answered, "The waterways didn't directly travel to the sea and water was sometimes too shallow to float the timbers."

"That didn't sound like it always worked well." George commented.

"Why couldn't ya just keep selling the trees?" William asked, confused that they must not have more trees between here and the ocean.

"Didn't ya ever hear tell of The Mast Tree Riot?" Stephen questioned.

"Not really." William answered, trying not to sound too ignorant. He looked over at George who shook his head confirming it wasn't familiar to him either.

"Oh, my boys, that's when people really started to get riled up." Stephen readjusted his arm and lifted it off the counter, "Let's sit over by the fireplace I'm beginning to feel a chill. "

The trio shifted themselves and their tale to the flickering flames in front of the fire. George waited on one of the customers who needed change and directions to the Meeting House while William helped Stephen carry over his tankard to the end table.

"All the pine trees that were twenty-four inches in diameter and bigger were needed for masts, some were seven feet wide. They were reserved for the *King of England's ships* to hold up their sails. " He raised his drink sarcastically.

"That doesn't seem fair, why should England get them?" William asked indignantly.

"England got them because it was the law. Also included was a fifty pound fine for each tree cut that wasn't theirs."

What! But didn't the people settling here need those trees for their homes and barns?" William was really not liking this news.

"That was exactly the problem. They were still owned by the King, both the people and the trees; it was 1734."

"Ohhh!" The boys said in unison realizing the old man was talking about the time period of the War of Independence.

Stephen took a deep long swig of his drink and continued, "There was a Surveyor of The King's Woods, he was an officer that enforced the rules, along with his four deputies. They marked each and every tree they came across with a King's Arrow."

Stephen demonstrated the movement of the shape with his finger on top of the table face.

"Bet they weren't popular." George remarked.

"Got that right!" Stephen replied. "Some of the Colonists would cut their boards twenty inches wide and just hide or throw away the left-over tree."

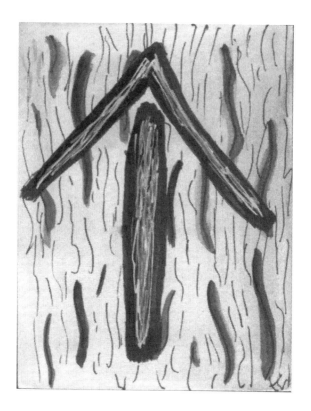

"Good for them. How were they ever gonna survive without the lumber? That wasn't right they couldn't use their own trees on their own land."

"One of the first battles between the Colonists and the Crown was when Surveyor General David Dunbar and his deputies went to Fremont. The frontiersmen got mad and burned down fifty square acres."

"Whoa, that's quite a lot." George commented while pondering the size of that in his mind.

Stephen went on, "It was a large area. Too bad too, a waste. Sheriff Whiting arrested Ebenezer Mudgett of Weare. While the deputies and the sheriff were waiting for Mudgett to get money for his fines they stayed at an inn. The sheriff and deputies awoke to be beaten with a small sapling switch on their bare backs and had the manes shaved off along with the tails and ears cut off their horses. They had to ride home in this condition. "

"That sounds like a hard time for those men." William said.

"It was a bad time, so much unrest between neighbors." Stephen added. "The sheriff returned with more men to help him. They caught eight of the offenders."

"Did they kill them?" George wondered and held his breath.

"Nope, just fined them twenty shillings, no jail time either. Four years later Patriots secretly gathered up those masts that were awaiting shipments to England and towed them back inland."

"Ya boys heard of the Tea Tax?" Stephen questioned the young men.

William nodded, "Sure, people talk about The Boston Tea Party, that what ya mean?"

George added, "Oh right, that's when they dumped all the tea into the harbor."

"Were you there?" William asked Stephen.

"No, but some of my family was." he answered. "Ya can't blame them for not wanting to pay any more taxes to the King, especially for services they weren't getting. No more giving and getting nothing. Taxation without representation."

That sounded familiar to both the boys. They had heard their family talk of their involvement with The Sons of Liberty many times.

"Ya do know that the first battle of The War of Independence was fought right here in New Hampshire. December 14th & 15th of 1774." Stephen informed the young men.

"My uncle always says it was Fort William and Mary. He was there. My neighbor's cousin in

Lexington doesn't agree. I always said it was true no matter what, I like the name, William." William stated proudly.

Stephen agreed "Your uncle is right. Fort William and Mary in New Castle. It was an area with a small island controlling the entrance to Portsmouth Harbor.

The fort was falling apart because at the time England didn't take care of it with those tax dollars we were talking about."

The boys now understood another situation where England was neglecting to care for the colony's properties and one more reason the citizens were unsatisfied with that government. "That sounds like another reason they didn't want to pay more tax." George realized aloud.

Stephen looked at George, "Wise boy, you are starting to catch on to that burning in the belly feeling of 'Not Right, Let's Fight Attitude'. British Naval Captain John Cochran and five soldiers ran the fort. Word was out that no powder or ammunition was to be exported to the Colonies anymore. William and Mary had some supplies, and our Sons of Liberty boys were going to get it." Stephen leaned toward William, "Tell your

14

neighbor's cousin in Lexington that a Silversmith and Patriot named Paul Revere was sent to tell the Patriots that England was taking control of all the forts. Paul went to Samuel Cutts, who later became the first governor of New Hampshire. I should know, Samuel was my family. Anyway, Paul was to tell the Patriots that the Brits were taking control of all Forts."

"I'm sure the cousin wouldn't change his mind, but I sure believe it." William told Stephen.

Stephen confirmed, "Do. Believe it. It is the truth. Riders set out to warn the citizens. Fife and drum marched out to sound the alarm. At least two hundred men, some said closer to four hundred, joined the Patriots. Governor Wentworth tried to warn Captain Cochran and his soldiers at the fort. Captain Cochran ordered the cannons and muskets to be fired. "

George looked concerned, "That sounds bad. "

"No one was injured from the cannons or the muskets. " Stephen painted a vastly different picture than the boys had envisioned. "We overpowered them before they could reload. The Patriots yelled 'Huzza, Huzza, Huzza!' and pulled

15

down the king's flag. But the Captain still wouldn't give up the keys to the powder magazine."

"Now, that could get him killed. Did it?" George asked.

Stephen replied, "No, it wasn't that important to hurt him, they just wanted the supplies. So, men took axes to the door and seized a hundred barrels of gun powder." He saw the boys looking at the gun powder keg in the tavern sizing them up in their mind. After he let them digest this information, he went on, "3,200 flints, five kegs of bullets and other supplies. You can thank the efforts of John Langdon for the first day's battle. The British tried to get men to protect the fort, but not one man would enlist. The captain was hoping to get at least thirty signed up. But, to our luck thirty or forty sons of liberty men went with the Patriot John Sullivan that night and seized the fort again. They took the remaining powder, sixty muskets, fifteen four-pound cannons, one nine-pound cannon, a large quantity of cannon shot and every other little scrap they could find. One cannon was too large to move."

"What'd they do with all that stuff?" William asked.

"Carried it off in flat bottom gundalow boats with Captain Cochran and his soldiers as prisoner. They floated up the Piscataqua River, the Great Bay, and Oyster River, they had to chop ice in the Great Bay."

"They split the supplies up between the towns of Durham, Exeter, Kingston, Epping, Nottingham, and Portsmouth."

William stated, "That was some quick work and thinking."

"As with all the Patriot endeavors, we were quick on our feet and scrappy." Stephen proudly announced. "Some say, there's still a cannon in one of these town churches to this day."

"Which one?" George questioned.

"Don't know." Stephen answered, "If I did, I would have gotten it years ago."

"Makes sense." William noted.

George wanted to know, "What happened to the fort?"

"The Brits got it eventually. I guess we couldn't get it in good repair and man it. All they got was an empty unsafe building. Not long after that General Wentworth hopped on the Scarborough boat, went to the Isles of Shoals, issued his last proclamation, and sailed to Boston. New Hampshire was no longer subject to the king of Great Britian."

He ended his story and took himself out of the wooden booth seat.

The boys realized that they had just had another real conversation with Old Man Stephen. Now they didn't want him to leave, but they had to get home and do their chores.

Stephen looked back as he opened the door to leave and said, "But that was just the start of a revolution. One worth the fight. Night boys." With that the door shut behind him.

CHAPTER THREE: ONLY 15

The next morning on their way to school, George questioned Stephen meeting up with him on his walk to town, "You were only fifteen?"

Stephen chuckled, "Yup. You can't get over that can ya, boy?"

"I even asked my family about that; they said you were probably closer to eighteen."

Stephen started shaking his head and talking, "My boy, it was a different time then. My family were struggling farmers. This hilly granite-filled ground made farming tough. We were good at being lumbermen but when that came to a halt, we had to find another way to make a living. Farming became our only option." Stephen paused. Then added, "All the men at the Meetinghouse signed up for 'the cause' that day, even some of the elderly and lame."

Stephen spoke on as the boys had hoped, they didn't want him to notice how they had made a quick glance toward his arm. But Stephen looked right at it and continued, "That left only the woman and children to care for the crops and hearths. We had many mouths to feed in my household when I joined the cause, I felt guilty if I left or stayed." He started counting on his fingers, "My mother, my father, Susan, Elizabeth, & Uncle Johnny Cake. All under one roof. "

They giggled and said under their breath, "Uncle Johnny Cake! "

"That was my mother's nickname for her baby brother. He loved cornbread and was named John." Stephen added with a smirk.

George questioned, "We always hear 'say your prayers'. Weren't people praying enough to stop the war?"

"Do you know a prayer strong enough to stop a war? Sometimes God answers prayer in his own way and time, it usually isn't our plan."

George stopped to hit a rock with a stick across their path, "You were only 15." shaking his head to still try to understand.

"I wanted to join before the war was over."

George's eyes widened, "To be in a real battle. How lucky. "

"Lucky?!" Stephen sternly raised his voice.

"But you wanted to join. "

Stephen stopped in his tracks, "Understand, it was war. You do not know what it is like to almost shoot one of your own men. Once a boy kills a man, even to save his own life, he can never take that back. You will never be the same. King George III encouraged his officers to help themselves to any of our property. They captured the landowner's house servants and made them slaves. Called them soldiers for their side. The sight of a sea of red in our fields of green and gold is never forgotten. They would burn our homes, barns, and kill the children. Do you know what it is like to bury a community of the dead? An enemy can be cold-blooded," he paused, "and sometimes it wasn't just the enemy, but even one of your own that was this brutal. It was serious, not a game!"

An uncomfortable silence fell upon the trio. George was filled with shame that he was named George. George was a family name, but he always had resentment when it would relate to the tyrant king.

"I hate having the name George! "

William tried to console him, "No shame, it was the name of Washington, as well. "

Stephen, being the gentleman he was, inhaled a deep breath, started walking, "You didn't mean any harm by your questions. I'm sorry I got a little hot. The youth can't learn from mistakes of the past unless we tell and teach them. "

The young men seemed relieved knowing he was not upset.

William questioned, "Did you move here by yourself?"

He reminded them, "Remember, I had some family in Seville. Relatives of the man who went to the mill in the snowstorm. They put my dad up for a while and he farmed and built his own cabin. It wasn't too big but at the time it was just him. Then he sent for my mother and started their family here. We returned to the coast a few times after that for important family events. It was a long trip."

George took a breather and leaned against an oak tree, "What'd ya think of the coast? What was it like?"

William piped in, "Yassir, we've never been there."

"Many nights I sit here in these beautiful woods and still a piece of me longs for the sea. I pray God will forgive me and not be angry that I am not fully satisfied with my blessings." He bowed his head and looked back up. "The tide comes and goes every day and night. The cresting and falling of the waves are endless. The taste of sea salt will never quench a thirst but can have a healing power. The smell of a sea breeze is all its own. It is so different there. It is worth the journey to the coast." He pointed a finger at them and said, "But never trust the power of the sea's undertow it's apt to be as dangerous an enemy as its healing powers are to repair a soul's longing for a certain peace."

William consoled Stephen, "Sorry your family had to leave the sea."

They all continued their travel.

Stephen reassured them, "Thanks Lad, my family was good at logging, as I told ya, but farming was a struggle. We tried other ways to make money and survive. Our luck we knew Captain John Stark and the Rogers Rangers from the Fort Number 4 crew who fought in the French and Indian battle. They knew every inch of these woods, knew how to scout, scavenge, and to even use a tomahawk.

"Ya ever hear tell of the secret Culper Spy Ring?" Stephen inquired.

"Nope." The boys said in unison.

Stephen leaned in, putting his fingers to his lips, and whispered, "Shhh. Cause it's a secret." Stephen looked around behind him in the bushes, "You never know when a neighbor could turn on you. Be it a Spy, Loyalist, or Tory. Tory Hole was just a couple towns over." He pointed to the Northwest.

"We need to know this!" George said excitedly rubbing his open palms back and forth.

"Next time boys I need to get into town and get some supplies. Don't you have school today?" as he headed on his route to the store.

"We do!" William shouted. The boys continued to the schoolhouse, picking up their pace and waving goodbye to Stephen. They were late now and would have to do chores for the teacher after school.

CHAPTER FOUR: SPIES, LIES, & PATRIOTS

William's father was ill and in bed with the whooping cough. The family was quite worried. Lately, William had to do his share of the chores and more. He hadn't seen Stephen for a while and was very anxious to hear more of his war tales. Especially details of the dangling Spy Story, he had left them with on their walk to school. The neighbor, Anne, had come to help with laundry and meals so Ma could tend to the animals. George and he had made plans to help Maribelle, the owner of The Stumble Inn Tavern.

Stephen wasn't much older than them when he fought. The boys couldn't imagine being at war but strangely were a little more curious about it now.

George dropped by to ask William about his dad and if he could go to the tavern today. It was a go, so they started off.

"I spy Stephen!" George pointed.

William joked back in the voice of a pirate, "Aye, Spies are what we be talking about, Matey."

The boys didn't bother the old soldier right away as he was talking with another man, and they knew that it would be rude to interrupt. The man looked to be about Stephen's age.

Stephen spotted them and motioned for them to come over. When the boys approached, he said, "Can you bring us a couple drinks?" He pointed toward the other man and said, "Thomas here thinks he can finally win a game of checkers against me."

"Sure can." George questioned. "The usual?"

Stephen nodded, "Yes."

Thomas piped in, "Don't think it. Know it." and went back to look at the pieces in deep thought of his next move.

"That'll be a first!" Stephen jested with a wink.

Each boy brought a drink over. Stephen looked at the boys. He could tell they didn't know if they should ask about the spy story in front of his company. He knew he had left them wondering.

"You boys needing something?" he asked.

William answered, "Ah, not really if this is a bad time."

"Thomas, last I talked to these young men they were about to learn of the Culper Ring of Spies." He moved one of his checkers to another square.

So, George asked what had been on his mind. "Were any spies as young as sixteen?"

Stephen glanced at George and then back to the game contemplating his next move and replied, "Nope. Some were my age."

The boys had no idea Stephen's age and knew that it would definitely be rude to inquire. Luckily, he didn't care if they knew.

He leaned their way and said clearly and slowly, "Some were 60 and beyond."

The boys tried to not act surprised but couldn't imagine that an old man was a soldier, let alone a spy. They didn't know many men that age now, never mind ones that were ready for battle.

Thomas added to the discussion, "Each town needed to have men ready for militia and their own supplies." Remembering the order of equipment needed, he motioned around his body to where these items would be. While holding a rifle stance he said, "We needed our own musket and bayonet." While tapping his back he said, "A knapsack. " Patting his hip he said, "A cartridge box, a pound of powder, about twenty bullets and a dozen flints. "

Stephen contributed to the list as he added each item, "And each town had to always have ready: a barrel of powder, pounds of lead, and flints for every man. Along with anything else a man was lacking from his own home."

Thomas said, "We were at the ready with a ditty bag always packed. Needed to be ready in a minute."

"Minute Men!" the boys said looking at each other.

The older men just nodded.

Stephen held his checker and waved it toward the boys, "What do ya know about spies?"

"Know you're not a good one if you got yourself hanged!"

"That's a good start." Slowly a smile crossed Stephen's face as he was amused by the comment.

Thomas solemnly said, "Sadly that's what happened to Nathan Hale."

"Did ya know him? Were you friends? Were you a spy?" Then George realized he may have been too excited.

"You can ask." Thomas dryly replied, "We don't have to answer." He added with a wink, "That's what makes a good spy, Laddy."

The boys didn't know what he meant by that. Was he a spy? Is he still one? Was he joking?

The boys were now looking at the old soldiers with a new perspective.

Thomas continued, "Secret messages were sewn into buttons. Newspaper advertisements were in code."

Stephen said, "Patriots and Loyalists wrote their letters in code with invisible ink or as mask letters."

George said proudly, "Hey, William, we have done a secret code before."

"We have." Using his hand to cover his face William asked, "But, what's a mask letter?"

"Not mask like to wear on your face." Thomas explained. "A mask like to cover over parts of something. It was a top sheet to go over a regular letter. It had a shape cut out to reveal the real message. Only the words left to read was the secret message."

This made sense to the boys now. William went to get a couple of pieces of paper from the kindling box and got out his jackknife. "Could you show us?" he asked handing the paper to Thomas assuming it might be a more challenging task for Stephen to do one handed.

Thomas continued his story while making a shape in the paper. "Spies were working on both sides, the British and the Patriots, even some against their own spies. It was an unsettling and untrusting time. You do know that, even the Great General George Washington himself was once a long time Officer in the British Army. He at one time was working for George II from England against the French and the Indians." He allowed that to sink into the boy's mind for a minute. "The father of our country was at one time a loyal fighter for the country he went to war against. " That now made more sense to the boys. How families would be divided as to be true to England or be true to the Colonies. The Colonies then were known as America but still owned by England. So much has happened to change their country since that time.

"That's where it gets confusing. We needed the French to help us win the war. We had to trust them." Stephen said while making the last move on the checkerboard to win the game. "King Me!" he laughed!

"Dang! Thought I had this game for sure." Thomas mutteringly admitted his defeat. "Maybe if I wasn't explaining the war and cutting out a mask letter box, I would have beaten you!"

"Nope, not taking any of those excuses either. But those are some new ones." Stephen chided.

"Weren't the Sons of Liberty friends with the French? See that's the thing that doesn't make sense to me."

"That's what made this war so difficult. There were Patriots, Tories, Loyalists and Spies and they all could all be in one family. Some believed saying nothing made ya guilty. I felt actions not mere words proved your character."

"But, then men like British Lord Cornwallis who fought as a gentleman. He considered the enemy to also be his brother under God." Stephen made the boys really see how the sides could get muddy.

William wondered, "Okay you said, Spies. That I want to know about. Did you know any? What tricks did they do?"

Maribelle had snuck up right behind the boys. "Tricks? You know any tricks to make you work today? Any of you got a problem earning your pay?" She was holding a tray of dirty plates and tankards.

"Oh, sorry, sure Maribelle. We'll get right back to work." the boys scrambled.

"That'll be good of ya." she said waving her hand in the air and walking toward the dry sink to wash the dishes. Mumbling she continued, "We ain't putting on the dog or nothing. But, tidying up a tad, would be okay."

The boys quickly went about cleaning, sweeping, drying the dishes, and putting them away, tending to the fire, stacking firewood, and filling the kindling box.

When William returned, he said to the men, "I want to know about the Culper Ring."

"Could you please, kindly tell us? Was Nathan Hale one of them?"

"No, he wasn't, but his friend and classmate, Benjamin Tallmadge was."

George broke in and stood tall, "Give me liberty or give me death!"

William corrected him, "I have but one life to give to my country."

Stephen sipped his drink and waited for them to finish. The boys were swarming around like mosquitoes. It didn't bother him that their youthful energy had interrupted his story, but it was inaccurate.

He calmly said, "Gentlemen, first of all, at the young age of nineteen Nathan was captured as a spy and hanged. He was quoted before his hanging saying, 'I regret that I have but one life to give for my country'. The quote, 'Give me liberty or give me death' was Patrick Henry, another man, another story."

"Oh yeah. " William remembered, "Wasn't Patrick Henry from Pennsylvania?"

"Yup, think so." George was brushing off William and turned to the men, "Please tell us your spy story."

Thomas said, "Not actually our spy story."

Now the boys didn't know if the guys were or were not involved. That spy business was tricky.

Stephen began the long-awaited tale, "Benjamin Tallmadge was a classmate of Nathan Hale at Yale. In 1778 Ben became a Major in the Continental Army. General George Washington made him the head of the Continental Secret Service."

The boys settled down for this one. Spies, secrets, and patriots all in one story. This had to be good.

"Was Tallmadge Mr. Culper?" George asked.

"Good Guess but no. Samuel Culper was the code name for a farmer named Abraham Woodhull." Thomas answered.

William asked, "Why didn't they just say Abraham Woodhull?"

Stephen replied, "Wouldn't have been much of a secret spy to use his real name."

"Of course, wonder why they'd use Culper? Do the letters stand for something?" William pondered.

Stephen said, "Well they needed a code name and Washington chose Culpepper. Woodhull wanted it shortened to Culper. "

George whacked William on the arm, "Stop asking for the little details. I want the meat of the story!"

"There was even a Culper Junior later on in the story and not his child. This story has spies, secret names, codes, plots, and plans." Stephen teased while excusing himself to use the outside privy.

"Even had a woman involved." Thomas added nonchalantly while chewing on a chunk of roll.

George blurted, "Not true!"

"Actually quite a few women." Stephen noted returning with a crisp apple for each of them. "When the men were encamped in such places as Valley Forge, they had their camp followers. They were often wives and children. The women would usually cook, clean, do laundry and mending and such. But there were a few who would risk life and limb. Such things as writing and delivering secret messages. Some through such things as innocent as hanging out the laundry to dry. A pattern of different colored laundry in a certain order was a way to say what cove or tree a message or package was dropped off." He continued, "One was Anna Strong, another Mary Woodhull, and a slave named Abigail. Some of those women were even the British officer's wives."

"That all sounds pretty dangerous." The boys made a sweep of the tavern for any of the patrons' needs before joining the older gentlemen again.

Thomas continued, "Well remember the British and Colonist were on the same side during the French and Indian War. It came upon the colonists to quickly choose to be a Loyalist or a Patriot. Some of the British soldier's wives were born in the colonies. Their family was on the ground that their English fighting husbands were lobbing cannonballs at. General Washington needed some intelligence. He needed to find out what the Brits were doing. Remember being that he was a loyal servant to good old England just before, he still had some connections to the Loyalists and Tories. Of which he took full advantage." He took a bite of his apple.

"Sounds like they had counter, counter, counter spies." William said while twirling his finger in circles like a tornado.

William and George picked up the men's dirty dishes and apple cores. They walked the dishes to the cleaning sink and threw the apples out back in the pig slop pail. William refreshed the drinks while George stoked the fire. The tavern was beginning to fill up with customers and they knew they would have to take a break from the spy tale soon.

Thomas continued, "Woodhull, Tallmadge, and Anna were all trusted childhood friends. Also in their circle was Caleb Brewster. Brewster was a whaler and a lieutenant in the Continental Army. He would sail his ships across the Long Island Sound to Fairfield, CT. Robert Townsend, who owned a boardinghouse, would gather information in New York City and give it to Woodhall. Woodhall would tell Anna. Anna would hang a black petticoat on the clothesline as a signal to Brewster that there was a message. Then she would hang a pattern of different colored handkerchiefs to say which cove or tree trunk to find it. Brewster who would in turn share with Tallmadge, then on to the main man himself, Washington. It also was done in reverse, Washington on down the line."

"That's a lot to remember!" William said.

"Just the beginning." Stephen added, "The spies also had their New York City contact in the Print Shop. The owner would run an advertisement with a secret code. All The Sons of Liberty to know the code and what the message really said."

"Of course. All these pieces had to flow together. A broken link in the chain was a ruined plan." Thomas agreed. "Culper would go to the seaport listen in on the conversations of the officers and take notes of the English Navy such as how many of their soldiers were entering and leaving the city and where they were going."

"How could he get away with that? Didn't they see him taking notes?" William asked.

"As a spy, he had a cover. He was just a farmer; trading produce for meat. He may say he was visiting his sister. Or take Anna Strong as a "wife" because they were less suspicious of married couples. He wrote and hid his notes with invisible ink. They never thought different." He got up, stretched his legs, took a few steps, and came back to the table. "There was also Austin Rowe who helped some, especially when Woodhall was ill."

George said, "This is so interesting. Any of them ever get hung?"

"Not a one." Stephen noted. "The spies from Setauket, New York were strong Patriots and had many reasons to be angry with the British forces. They turned Tallmadge's father's church into a horse stable, taking over the homes and businesses as their own."

Thomas said, "A Word about Spies. Spies worked on both sides the British and the Patriots, even some against their own spies. It was an unsettling and untrusting time. Remember we said, Washington was an English Officer. That's where it all gets muddled."

"Are we talking about the traitor Benedict Arnold?" George questioned.

"Traitor to some, hero to others. He had no reason to go against his brothers, he was one of them. Arnold is always remembered as a traitor, but do you know at one time he was a fierce Patriot fighting in the early years of the American Revolution? He fought at Lexington, with Ethan Allen to help capture Fort Ticonderoga and was made a Colonel. He was a Brigadier General in George Washington's Army. During The Battle of Saratoga Arnold was one of the main characters to stop British General Johnny Burgoyne. He just always felt like he got the short end of the stick when it came to being recognized by the Patriots. During the battle at Freeman's Farm in Saratoga Arnold's leg was severely wounded in a battle on horseback. He limped in pain the rest of his life."

Thomas added, "Never mind he fell in love with Margaret 'Peggy' Shippen." The boys made a face when he said love.

"Yuck. Girls." George sputtered. William shushed him. Love was yucky but he wanted more of the story even if he had to hear a little of those gushy lovey dovey details.

Thomas continued, "But she was a Loyalist half as old as him." He looked at George and said, "But this is where spies come in again. She was in love with John Andre. Does the name Andre sound familiar?"

"The British spy that was hung? He had West Point Papers from Arnold, maybe?" William asked.

"Correct!" Thomas confirmed. "Andre knew that Arnold was not happy, and he convinced Peggy to marry him even though many people think she was not in love with him. Arnold got faced with a court martial for spending the public's money. He resigned his post. After the resignation Arnold began writing to John Andre cause his wife told him to. Andre was the Chief of the British intelligence. "

William blurted, "We know no good can be coming from that! "

Thomas continued, "Arnold also had stayed close with George Washington so he could get the important information. Over the next few months Andre and Arnold kept talking and he agreed to hand him over information that would destroy Washington and the Patriots. He decided to hand over control of West Point. Arnold weakened the defensives, even removed an over 60-ton chain from the river made to stop British ships! Andre and Arnold then met in person. He gave him the information. Andre was caught and Arnold's letter was found."

Stephen added, "George Washington was heartbroken. How could this man have treated him like this?"

George said, "William, I could never do that to you. " William nodded.

Stephen continued, "Benedict Arnold escaped to Britain. He was protected from punishment. He was a decorated Patriot for years and died shamed in London. Andre was executed for spying. Hung."

Thomas added, "Imagine a Brigadier General at one time and a traitor in the end. Benedict Arnold was out for himself. Washington was fighting for justice. That our boys was the difference."

Clang, Clang, Clang. It was three o'clock. William should have been home an hour ago. It was past his time.

"I gotta go!" William nervously announced. "My ma will have my hide if I don't get home."

"I got chores, too!" George called.

"That's alright boys. Git along. I still got to take this guy's king back. " Stephen was pointing to Thomas. "We have a serious wager."

"That you'll soon be losing, my friend." Thomas answered.

The boys scrambled home with the spy tales swirling in their minds.

CHAPTER FIVE: FAMILY LINES

William got right to his chores when he got home. His family hadn't noticed him being so late. His dad was feeling better and had joined the family for dinner that night. William was so glad to see him on the mend, but he still had all the spy details spinning in his head. He brought the subject up. "What do you all know about spies?" and shoved a heaping spoonful of mashed potatoes in his mouth.

"Flies? Don't tell me they are in my custard pie!" Grammie Lang started swatting in the air.

"Not Flies, Grammie, SPIES!" He said clearer and louder for her to understand. They had a great relationship and she always made him laugh.

She stopped in her tracks and said with a raised eyebrow, "Spies, like that scoundrel Benedict Arnold?"

Dad grumbled under his breath, "Benedict Arnold..."

Mom abruptly interrupted, "Alexander, I know how you feel about him. I agree that I dislike how he ended his life." She paused, "But what about Saratoga?"

"Saratoga he should have lost his life there, not just crippled his fool leg. That gutless traitor. I know he was a friend of your family, but really Betsy, he wasn't worth the cost to ship him back to his motherland. " He ended looking her way.

"Alex, have you forgotten he wasn't recognized for his great courage at Fort Ticonderoga and then again at Saratoga?" Betsy said sympathetically.

"There is never a good excuse to set up the plan of trapping and killing of your own friends, I guess unless you are the High and Mighty Great Benedict!" William's father raised his voice along with his pointed finger to the sky. Then there was an awkward pause.

Betsy picked up her plate with a, "Hmph!" and walked to scrape her scraps into the compost bucket.

Alexander went back to eating and William could tell they had had this disagreeable conversation before. He also surmised his grandmother agreed with her son.

A few minutes later Betsy came back and refilled Alexander's cider and gave him a second helping of his venison sausage. She placed her hand on his shoulder and said in a soft voice, "You know, I think he was wrong."

"I know." Alexander put his hand on hers.

William's little sister Hannah Rose asked, "What happened to his leg?" Sometimes a seven-year-old doesn't know when it was the best time to not ask a question. William just kept his head down and ate. He was interested in his family's differing opinions on the subject. His parents usually agreed on situations. This made more sense of Stephen and Thomas' story of families having different opinions of the war.

Alexander took a deep breath, "I will tell you the story. It really is a sad tale. Arnold was a Hero."

William lifted his head, "I didn't know you thought he was a hero, Dad?"

"I said WAS. Benedict Arnold was a fierce Patriot against the Stamp Act. He was with Ethan Allen when they captured Fort Ticonderoga. A Proud Son of Liberty!" Alexander stated.

William said, "Old man Stephen and his friend told us all about the Spies. "

"Did they tell ya at Saratoga he stopped the British taking over?"

Betsy interrupted imitating Alexander's voice, "Saratoga the Turning Point of the Revolutionary War! "

Alexander quickly replied, "That it was, woman. Arnold's leg was severely injured in the Saratoga Battle. It was his second injury to that leg. Arnold wanted to continue to oversee battlefield troops but, General Washington thought Arnold needed more healing time."

"Gates got the glory." Grammie Lang interrupted slicing and serving them pie.

Alexander said, "He was no better!"

Grammie Lang chimed in "Freeman's Farm, Bemis Heights, Stillwater. All these names mean the Great Battle of Saratoga, ya know. It took place on the west bank of the Hudson River just north of Albany. It had British, Germans we called Hessians, Canadians, Indians, and Loyalist Americans all against the American Colonists. It was quite the fight." She pointed out the window as if lining them up, and continued, "There were Morgan's men on horseback and our own New Hampshire Regiments with Major Dearborn, Colonel Cilley and Colonel Scammel." The Grandmother took a sip of tea. "When the militia left the homes and farms to defend the country the children's chores increased greatly and many boys also became the man of the house. The meals could become lean if the woman and children were in charge of everything."

Alexander added, "This Battle did change the course of the war." He looked at his wife. They smiled. "Here's where some of your spies and lies come into this story. John Andre was the Head of Intelligence for the British. He had an ally named Margaret "Peggy" Shippen. "

William said, "They told us about her. She was trouble."

His father mumbled under his breath, "Most woman are." And smirked at his wife. She gave him a stern look then grinned.

William's one-year older sister Phebe sat down clenching her drying towel to her chest and with a sigh said, "It really was a sad, sad, love story."

She and her classmates had discussed this situation before.

One of his older brothers Daniel looked at her and said, "Ahhhh Maaaa, please don't tell that dribble."

Sweet Hannah Rose got all dreamy eyed and said, "Mama, don't leave out a detail."

Betsy assured them, "Oh don't you worry boys, it also has spies and hanging. If you are interested." As she walked past them. This got the attention of all the kids: William, Phebe, Hannah Rose, Daniel, and the oldest brother Henry, who had never even made a peep during the whole meal because he never talks to any of the family if he can get away with it.

William said, "Mom I heard a lot of it, but would like to know more and share it tomorrow with George at the tavern."

"Did you forget tomorrow is the Sabbath? It is also our turn to have the Pastor over for dinner. Remember George Washington was known quoting about the 'Divine Providence'. That was how he often referred to God."

William had forgotten tomorrow was Sunday, but he would catch up with George as soon as he could.

"We all need to get comfortable for this story." Grammie Lang said. "And we need more pie!"

Alexander said, "Not right now for me, think I'll go check on the animals. Henry, you want to join me?"

Unexpectedly Henry replied. "After this story, Dad."

The family was shocked. Even Henry wanted these details. Alexander put down his coat and said, "I might as well have pie."

Betsy loved having her whole family by her side and sharing in a good storytelling. Seemed like it had been ages since they all shared a few moments together. Henry was very distant as he got older and wished he didn't live in the countryside. He thought he'd have so many more opportunities for him off the mountain. William was often gone with school and the tavern. Daniel and Phebe were around to help with the main household chores, but they would find time to fish and play away from the house. Hannah Rose was getting older and often didn't even want to be read to sleep anymore. She looked around and just soaked it in.

They were all together.

Betsy continued her tale of love and drama, "Peggy and Andre were in love."

Alexander interrupted, "That's rumor and hearsay, you know what The Bible says about that!"

Betsy just brushed him off.

"Gross! Not this part, again." William said, turning his head away.

"Vile, just Vile!" Daniel said as he wolfed down his pie.

"Hang in there." Betsy continued while Hannah Rose pulled her chair over and snuggled in the crook of her mother's arm. "They were in love, but Andre also loved his country and the crown. He knew Arnold had known the Shippen family, so he wanted Peggy to write love letters to Arnold. He wanted her to get Arnold to fall in love with her and convince him to come to the British side. She knew he was so neglected by Washington and the rest of the army. She was to find out some of the Continentals' secrets. Peggy's love for Andre was so deep she agreed to do it."

Hannah Rose sighed, "Oh, love, Mama please continue." William just looked at her shaking his head in disgust.

Henry said, "I stuck around for this." and started to get up.

Alexander put his hand on Henry's shoulder and escorted him back into the chair, "Sit down. Where are your manners? Let your mother finish her story. "

"Thank you, dear."

Grammie Lang wiped her mouth with a cloth napkin, "It worked so well, they married."

Betsy continued, "But it seemed like everyone lost to me. Peggy and Andre were in love. Benedict got a woman who did not love him. It all seems sad. "

"Sounds like they were all liars." Henry said while stretching in his chair. "Maybe they all deserved what they got!"

"Did Andre deserved to be hanged?" Betsy asked as she watched Daniel place his hands around his neck wide-eyed.

Daniel blurted out, "He was hanged and not Benedict? Benedict was the spy against us! Oh no wait, they both were."

"That's why I have no use for the three of them, or any sympathy." Their dad piped in, "William, did they talk about the Turtle?"

"An animal that was a spy? No!" William answered.

His father laughed out loud and slapped his knee. "Can you imagine a slower animal to be a quick-witted spy?" asked Alexander. "No, no, it was an underwater boat. "

Henry blurted out, "You're kidding us!"

Daniel said, "Really Dad, don't tease us. No one can hold their breath and fight underwater. "

"I'm telling ya the truth." Alexander answered. "The Turtle was no animal but was a battle tool that went underwater. It was a one-man craft that was hand powered. "

"Did it look like a turtle?" one of the children asked.

"It was kinda the shape, so turtle was a good code name for it. They had hoped to use it to quietly attach a mine to the enemy ship, The Eagle, in New York Harbor."

"Did it blowup? Did it work?" Hannah Rose asked, biting her nails.

"No honey, it actually didn't. There were some problems with this set up. It was only 8 feet long and could only hold one person. The man that invented knew the craft best but wasn't the best man to operate it. Every bomb missed and exploded nearby, but luckily no one was injured. "

"Wow what a story. Imagine underwater warfare." William said. "Wait until I share this one at work."

"It would sure be better than that bomb about Peggy and Benedict and LOVE!" Daniel said with a sarcastic voice and danced around the room. "Yuck!" he announced with a gag motion. "Come on Dad, I'll help you with the chores in the barn." All the other men folk walked out of the kitchen to their evening work.

CHAPTER SIX: VALLEY FORGE

William entered the Tavern eager to add his new spy information about the Turtle. The owner Maribelle told him and George to get out and go do something, maybe go fishing. There were no customers that day and she couldn't pay them if she had no income. So, they happily went fishing.

George went to gathering up some live maggots from the pig slop bucket and William got to digging up a handful of worms underneath the compost pile. Maribelle always had a few cane poles with hooks lined up by the brooms in the corner. If the boys got a big enough keeper fish, she would give them a haypenny. If not, they could always bring home fresh fish to fry for dinner that night. The boys were excited to have a relaxing time and catch up on their thoughts of the latest conversations about the war, and especially William who could talk about the Turtle. They didn't waste much time getting to the bank of the pond. It was a popular fishing spot during that time of year.

Before they could bait a hook, they heard, "Well, don't great minds think alike! What you young laddies doing here during your work time? Playing hooky?" It was Stephen.

Both boys stood up and greeted him. "Nice to see ya!" George said. William added, "Nope not hooky, Maribelle kicked us out today, no customers."

"Care if I join you on the log?" Stephen questioned.

"Please do!" William said brushing some leaves and dirt off the dead fallen tree.

Stephen set down his fishing bag and bait can.

"My family had a conversation about the Turtle. Do you know about it?"

"You ain't got turtle." George quipped back.

Stephen said, "Oh sure." As he continued prepping for fishing. "You talking about the underwater bomb?"

"Whoa, whoa. What am I missing?" George said confused.

William retold the entire family conversation. He didn't miss a detail. George was extremely excited to learn all the new spy information. The more he knew the more he wanted to know.

Stephen said, "It was a bold and dangerous move by those men. It's a shame it didn't work but fortunately there were no serious injuries or deaths. "

William asked Stephen, "Were you with Washington when he crossed the Delaware?"

"That I was not."

"But I was at Valley Forge camp and that is a whole other tale."

"We got time. What was it like?" George asked, jigging his line, and hoping to hear another story.

Stephen started in, "Every day was horrific. Think of one of the worse meals you ever ate and think of now having to eat it every day, every meal."

"That sounds kinda awful." George said.

"It was. Did you ever eat a burnt leaf?" Stephen asked.

William gave him a puzzled look, "Can't say that I have."

Stephen went on, "That was my main meal and usually dirt would blow in the pot. We were hungry, cold, and dirty."

William asked, "Didn't you have all those women and children to cook and clean for you, the camp followers?"

Stephen replied, "Can't cook up what ya don't have. We were supposed to have beef, pork, and fish. Things like rice, cornmeal, and flour. Also, some rum and whiskey. Measly meals don't compare or sustain ya. We left our jobs, homes, and families. We traveled that vast wilderness and had none of our basic needs met. Burnt leaves. Remember when Thomas and I told ya how much each minute man needed for his own belongs? This war went on for 8 years and 8 months and New Hampshire men served throughout."

"Why would anyone stay?" George inquired.

He answered, "Where ya gonna go? It was freezing and winter and you had no food, maybe not even shoes to travel. If you had your honor, you didn't desert the others. I went with my cousin. We were there on a mission and together."

"Where's your cousin live now?" William was curious as he didn't think he heard tell of this man.

Stephen took a breath and said, "His name was Benjamin. There were even worse things than being cold, dirty, and hungry. Back then, at Valley Forge, I was wishing those unfortunate events would change soon for all of us. That it would soon end. We were lucky enough that night to have some water and a fire cake. We had finally bunked down in our cramped and smoky tent for a few hours of shut eye. It had been a rough week. Many of the men had come down with the Smallpox. They were itching and sick. I went to talk to my cousin Benjamin who was sharing my corner of the cabin and the same wool blanket. He wasn't itching anymore. Lucky for him, he finally fell asleep. But he was a heavy snorer, and I should be hearing a sound similar to a wild boar snorting. Then a dreaded feeling overwhelmed me. He wasn't itching or snoring because he was dead. I said, 'Oh, dear God, Benny is dead.' I know he starved to death. He couldn't eat or take a drink for days. I felt numb for a few moments until I needed to scratch. Scratch like there was no end to it. I wanted to scratch that itch right off my body. I still wanted the itch to end but not like Poor Benny. 'Be careful what you wish for Mama use to tell me."

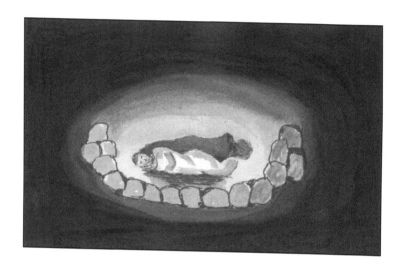

Stephen continued his heart wrenching tale and the boys hung on every word as they were living it themselves. "I was praying and wishing for Benny back but that wasn't going to happen." The boys each just shook their heads and began to have a heavy heart and so much sympathy for Stephen. "I felt guilty that the right side of his body was still providing some warmth for my comfort. As I cried and prayed for his soul and mine, I selfishly drifted off into a slumber. I couldn't stay awake I was too weak. I just hoped I would wake up."

Stephen checked his hook and rebaited with a maggot this time. He dipped the line in the water turned to the boys and questioned, "Surprise ya to hear tell that a grown soldier shed tears?"

William sympathetically answered, "How could ya not?"

"I came in and out of being awake. The fever was high, and I was burning up. Then the cold chilled me to the bone, and I shivered until I thought I would shake the teeth right out of my head. I don't know if it was hours or days, but I awoke in another place. I was dreaming of mother braiding my little sister's hair. It was soothing to watch. I realized someone was grooming my own hair and face. The water was cooler than I had hoped for on my face it was kinda waking me up. A young woman came into view. I wasn't in my own quarters and my own tattered dirty clothes. I was in a house. It had lanterns and I could smell venison stew. I loved venison stew. I heard men coughing and some were vomiting. This all must be a dream. Or possibly I am dead. I looked on each side of me for Benjamin. 'Sip of water,' she offered and tipped a ladle toward my lips from her pail. 'Where?' was all that, I could squeak out for words. 'Potsdam.' She replied and hurried away carrying supplies to another patriot. He looked worse off than me. I didn't know if he was even still alive. I wanted to grab her arm and ask her more. But I was too weak. A bandaged old soldier hobbled by behind me. I reached for his sleeve, 'Where is Benny,' my voice gaining volume. He cupped his hand to his ear, 'What son?' I repeated, 'Where is Benjamin?' 'Don't rightly know, he hadn't come this way. 'He tried to comfort me by adding, 'Maybe he is still on base camp. 'The woman passed by again, 'Where was?' before I could finish, she said, 'You are off base camp and in the hospital unit. 'My cousin Benjamin?' I continued saying and searched around me. It was hard to lift any part of my body as it all felt heavy like lead. I struggled more, 'Benjamin! Can you hear me?' I had questions, 'What day was it?' 'Where was the army?' I blurted out loud and clear, 'Did he die?' That sounded cold and uncaring. I reworded my question to her, 'I am sorry was he okay and where was the army?' The nurse returned, patted my shoulder, and told me to be calm. This wasn't good for me in my condition. What condition was Benny in? Then I remembered our last night together. He was gone. He was dead. I said it aloud to myself. I knew it was true when we shared the blanket. I wished it wasn't so. But wishing changes nothing. The nurse's eyes were welded with tears. I just slowly turned my head. What would I tell them at home?"

Stephen took a break from his story and was quiet for a bit. They all just set in their thoughts as fisherman often do. The boys dreaming of conducting the Turtle and sympathy for their unexpected new friend, Stephen. Stephen was reliving some thoughts he had suppressed for years along with being content to be looking at a peaceful body of water at this time in his life shared with his new young friends.

William broke the silence, "I got a bite! It's a big one!"

After a struggle he pulled out a fair-sized perch. "Nice one, Will!" George complimented him.

"Thanks."

"Now it's your turn George. Go get one." Stephen encouraged an eager George.

Which George did in no time. It was a golden trout and quite a beauty. All three of them admired it for a while.

The time rolled on and Stephen knew he had to get a moving, so he announced he was leaving. He took another swig from his canteen and said, "Far be it for me to get skunked on fishing from you Scallywags! But I did! Such is the luck of my ancestors."

"You'll do better next time." George encouraged Stephen.

"Right as rain, my young friend. I am pleased to watch you both have a good catch."

"It wasn't too much of a battle catching them today." George commented.

Stephen advised, "Always pick your battles. Sadly, when confronted in a battle, best to fight 'cause surrender could still mean death or worse. Not a time gone by in all these years, that I don't think of Benny every time I see the Crown Point Road."

"What could be worse than death?" William solemnly asked.

"You got an imagination boy, use it." Stephen replied. "I am reminded of this wretched disease every day of my life." Stephen said as he packed up with his one good arm. It did look difficult to the boys to do everything with only the use of one arm. They also comprehended that he was here, and his cousin wasn't. Stephen and the boys waved goodbye and then he walked around the bend and out of sight.

That story was a little hard to settle with the boys. All of his stories were strong, but that one was real and hit home. What would William and George do without each other? How could one have imagined coming back without the other; If one had died and one had lived. They picked up their fishing supplies and fish in silence. William glanced at George and thought what would life be like without him? They had been cousins and friends their entire life. Maybe George was thinking the same. William hugged him instead of their secret handshake. George hugged back. Not another word was spoken as they both went on their separate ways home.

CHAPTER SEVEN: THE PRICE OF FREEDOM

William awoke in the early morning and found his grandmother sitting alone drinking a cup of tea. This wasn't unusual, she was usually the first one up. He heard a mourning dove cooing. It was kinda peaceful.

His grandmother greeted him, "Good Morning, Willie." The water is still hot. Pour yourself a cup of tea and please join me." She slid her chair back toward the table and away from the lamp. "We can enjoy a few minutes of the morning together." She said with a warm and welcoming smile.

William got his drink and joined his grandmother. They sat in silence for a bit. He noticed the page in the bible was still open to where she must have just read her morning scripture. That was a daily ritual. She broke the silence and leaned toward William, "Watcha thinking about? You young people always have some thoughts floating through your minds." She gave him some moments to gather his thoughts he'd like to share, as she got up and scooped out some beans from the bean pot. She searched around for a hunk of meaty salt pork for William's serving. Then she reached into the cookie jar and added the last of the molasses cookies to each helping.

As she set the breakfast down William said, "Grammie Lang, you know I have been talking a lot with Stephen at the Tavern. He has given us so much information about The War of Independence." He took a bite of his molasses cookie and chewed. He knew he could ask his grandmother anything and valued her opinion. "What was it like for the rest of you. You know, people that stayed behind and didn't go to war?"

Grammie Lang finished chewing her bite of beans and took a swallow of tea. "It was tough on everyone, child. Our entire world changed. You know how each of us in the family has our own daily chores to do? Adding in planting and harvest season when we are so tired at night, we don't know how we are going to get back up again to do it in the morning."

William shook his head. He knew too well what it is like to have done everything you need to accomplish, then adding more like bringing in the hay. What it is like to have the blistering sun beating down on you endlessly for hours.

Because you can't hay when it's raining. He commented, "Like haying. Gotta make hay when the sun shines."

"Sure do, you know." After a bite and chew of the molasses cookie, she added, "Well, now you have that and the jobs of two other people in the family."

William's eyes got huge, he couldn't imagine having to do his father's and one of his brother's chores in addition to all that he had to do plus the haying.

"I'd have to tend to all the animals," she put her hand up to count on her fingers, "chop the wood, head to town to get the supplies, do the morning and nightly milkings!"

"Gee, Grammie, how's a kid do all that?"

"Exactly, you get it! Not well and exhausted." She confirmed.

"So, for us girls, the younger boys, and the ladies at home we had all that to be shared plus making dinner, mending, sewing, baking bread, getting the eggs, tending to the babies, baths, and schooling. It was overwhelming at times."

They both sat in silence for a while as they finished their breakfast. That was a lot for William to process. He had glamorous versions of the battle stories growing up and now in the last few months he had learned so much about the other side of war. Now his imagination was playing the struggles and hardships that just weren't on the battlefield.

Gram continued, "Oh, honey, we missed each other every day but, especially on the Sabbath. One thing that helped was a lot of people had their faith. We were lucky enough here to have a preacher to keep our faith strong, but I know at times even the pastor's weakened during the conflicts. "

William glanced over to the Bible that his grandmother had been reading and knowing now why her faith was always important to her. William could understand this and missing family on the Sabbath. Every Sunday his family would do only the necessary chores to keep the animals tended to and the house running smoothly, but nothing extra, it was the day of the Lord. Then they would get ready for church service. They would start the baths even the night before for the younger ones, then put on their best Sunday clothes. They had to be out the door early because there was no excuse for being late. Every Sunday the Meeting House was for church worship, nothing else. His family would worship together with their cousins, aunts, uncles, and grandparents all sitting together. Everyone in the town would gather putting away their differences long enough to worship, sing hymns, and read scripture for those few hours. They then would go home to a meal that was spread out like a feast. The meal always had venison or rabbit for the main course. They would take turns eating at each other's homes. The topper was, they had a dessert. They didn't always have a sweet like a molasses pudding or cookie like they were having today. He was lucky it was

Monday and Gram had tucked a few aside. She had a sweet tooth.

Gram stated, "William, you talked about girls in the war.

Many of them played a vital role."

William replied, "Stephen told us about quite a few."

"Did he tell ya about Molly Pitcher?"

"Not really, was she the one at Monmouth?"

"That she was. Sweetie Molly Pitcher. It was not clear if her name was Pitcher or a nickname as she carried pitcher upon pitcher of water for the soldiers and cannons. Oh, you must admire her strength, they say when her man fell during the loading of the cannon, she walked right over him picked up where he left off and fired that cannon! Then tended to what needed to be done after. Monmouth was in the sweltering heat of June and the hottest of all conflicts. The soldiers had to keep cooling themselves down along all the cannons and putting out fires the whole time. Not just a man's war everyone on the battlefield would have to pitch into the fight."

Gram was trying to fill in the gaps for William, "I know, Stephen told you about Saratoga and that Benedict Arnold!"

"I know you do not like Benedict Arnold." He replied.

She started sputtering, "That I don't! Even if you get injured or hurt for the cause, of what you believe in, it is still your cause! He was a little bit on the whiny side when he decided it wasn't good enough that he needed to be put on a pedestal and admired! He didn't get the recognition he decided he deserved and then turned to the other side. A Traitor! I still can't make sense and justify that." She paused and gathered herself.

William asked another question to get her off Benedict. "I see the picture hanging up in the Meeting House. The one with everyone signing the Declaration of Independence of July 4 th. Anyone from New Hampshire?"

Gram started to get out carrots and a turnip to peel for today's meal. She set them down on the table with a couple of knives and said, "Artist can take liberty with their paintings. Do you know the last signature on that document was signed on August 2nd?"

"I didn't. It shows them all around a table and lining up to sign their names." William recalled.

Gram set down her turnip and said, "It doesn't show our own Josiah Bartlett the first brave delegate of the Continental Congress to vote for independence. He was also the second to sign

76

after John Hancock's big fancy signature." She then took her finger and signed his name big in the air.

William questioned, "That is a big signature, why?"

She answered, "Hancock was proud to sign his name." Gram quoted, "We hold these truths to be self-evident, that all men are created equal, that they are endowed by their Creator with certain unalienable Rights, that among these are Life, Liberty, and the pursuit of Happiness. It was risky business for all the signers. They pledged their lives, fortunes, and sacred honor. Of the 56 signers they were lawyers, merchants, farmers, plantation owners, they weren't soldiers. When they fought this cause. Some viewed the act as treason and could be hanged. Some of their homes were ransacked, even worse five were captured and tortured by the British. "

"Gram, we didn't know all this." William said scraping peelings into the slop bucket.

"A man named Dunlap made a couple hundred copies of the document. When General George Washington received his copy in New York the Revolution broke out and lasted for eight years. Eight years for our small town. We had people involved the entire time." Gram remembered.

Gram started cutting the turnip into chunks and putting the pieces in the stew pot. "It was said that these are the times that try men's souls. Well, it tried everyone's souls. It was the first and only fight I saw my parents have."

William never liked grown-ups to fight, it always made him feel uneasy. He realized his grandmother was bothered by such things as a kid herself. He started to think how much she knew about all that time and never once stepped on a battlefield.

Gram continued, "My dad had come home on a leave for a short break. Many of the soldiers by now were deserting and not returning, our dad wasn't one. He was tending the milking when he had gotten word that one of his best buddies was killed. He came into the kitchen extremely upset and spotted my mother's pewter tea pot. It was one of her pride and joys from her childhood. It had belonged to her great grandmother, given to her by grandfather when he had gone on a trip to England. Dad looked at that and saw the British.

British hands that had made that like the British hands that taken his friends life. He snatched the pot off the shelf and took it out to the barn. He melted it down and made musket balls. "

With his hands to his mouth William said, "Oh no. What did your mother do?"

She was screaming, "What are you doing? Give that back! He was shaking her off and yelling in her face. They killed him! They killed him! while shaking the tea pot. We had never seen my dad with anger. She looked at us crying children watching and must have thought this battle isn't worth fighting right now. She let him go out the door. As he slammed it behind him, she comforted us by stroking our hair, wiping our tears, and saying it was all going to be alright. We were hoping it was."

"Did your mom forgive him?" William asked.

"A couple of days after we were all having another quiet dinner. My dad was going back to fight. He announced it to the entire family including my mom. 'Six months ago, I was plowing a field and now I am plowing through mangled bodies. 'The lobster backs could target my family, kill, or burn my home down while I'm gone. I am sorry to your mother that I melted down one of her prize possessions. Please forgive me. If not, what am I fighting for?' My mother hopped right up and hugged that man so hard. Then the rest of us joined in and threw our arms around them both. We cried and laughed and had the best dinner in a long time."

William was relieved with the news. He had hoped the family conflict was resolved. "Grammie, I know about the Liberty Tree, Spies, the Turtle."

She pointed her index finger at him with authority, "No ideas about you and that friend of yours trying any underwater adventures."

"I promise." He answered. "I know you don't love snakes and it has something to do with independence. So why do we hang a snake flag?"

"You got that right. Snakes are good for nothing! The Don't Tread on Me flag represents a period in history when the United States was still fighting for independence from Great Britain. Christopher Gadsden designed the flag. He became a Brigadier General in the Continental Army from South Carolina and at that time was leading the Sons of Liberty. Esek Hopkins, head of the Navy, proudly flew the flag on the ship the

Alfred. Benjamin Franklin also made a cartoon in his paper, the Pennsylvania Gazette. He suggested the best way to thank the British for their practice of sending criminals to America would be to send some rattlesnakes back to them. Franklin used the snake's curves to show the coastline and was cut into eight sections to show the colonies. South Carolina was the tail, while New England was the snake head and underneath the snake were the strong words, 'Join, or Die.' It was a symbol of unity among the American colonies."

"That makes sense. That sounds like such an awful time." William commented.

"That it was. After Monmouth on to Stony Point, nicknamed 'The little Gibraltar'. Known to be one of the most important achievements of the war. Brigadier General Anthony Wayne planned a midnight surprise attack. It was cloudy and the moonlight was covered. That made it better for getting in and not being seen. They didn't use guns, just bayonets. They pulled down the flag and yelled 'The fort's our own! ' Stony Point We shall not be moved from this hill!"

"Do you know about the surrender?" William asked a little impatiently.

"They say the surrender in Yorktown was almost in total silence. All we could hear was the clink of the weapons as they landed one atop of another with the defeat of each of their men." Gram clinked the knife blades together. William closed his eyes as if he could picture each one hitting in his mind. "One after another. They had won the battle. Some of those little ole boys from Seville up against the mighty trained British Soldiers. They were the Victors. Yes, George Washington, Divine Providence."

This fact had weighed heaviest on William, and it was time to get it out. "Gram there is a part of the war that bothered me the most, I kinda can't shake it." Gram set all she was preparing down and wiped her hands on her apron to give William her full attention. "It was when Stephen shared his story about Valley Forge."

"Uh, Valley Forge." she said shaking her head with a serious face. "That was a tough one for Stephen, you know. I am surprised he brought it up and talked about it. What do you know?"

"Gram, he said his cousin died beside him and he had to stay with him till the night was over."

William looked at Gram, she was tearing up. "I never knew that. He told no one. I think you boys might have been one of the first people Stephen ever shared that with. He never talked about it with anyone, ever."

"EVER?" William was feeling shocked and very honored to have that privilege.

Gram said with great sympathy for her friend, "That must have just been horrific. Poor, man. I still miss his cousin to this day. He was a good friend of mine." She wiped a tear away with her apron.

William was wringing his sweaty hands and continuing with his retelling of Stephen's tale. He had the most somber look his grandmother had ever seen on him. An overwhelming feeling of grief for Stephen and everyone involved flooded over William. He began to cry.

Gram got out of her chair and threw her arms around her hurting grandson. He just leaned onto her shoulder and sobbed.

When he stopped, he said, "I can't imagine going somewhere without George, or my brother, or sister, or you." Then he started again.

Gram just let him have this moment. She handed him her hanky and he wiped his eyes and blew his nose. When things seemed better, Gram looked him in the eye and held his hands. "You, okay?"

He said, "I'm alright." catching his breath and sat back down in his chair.

Gram reminisced, "I remember him coming home without him. It was heartbreaking. They were cousins and best friends. You never saw one without the other. Stephen shut down. He didn't talk about it, the war, his cousin, he didn't really talk much at all. He just worked and that was hard enough with his injury. We all felt it was best not to bring it up to him because it would make his pain worse. But if we didn't talk about it was like Benny didn't exist or he never lived. Now I wonder if we should have just kept going and saying we loved him. That he was important. It was a tough one because if we were brought up by his name it might bring up the pain. Our memory is often all have people left with us and if we don't share, we are making them disappear."

William sadly said, "Coming back without him. I don't know how you move on."

Gram Lang's advice was, "You got two choices. You move on or you stay stuck in it. I think you must deal with whatever the situation brought you, your feelings. Pull out your demons, deal with them and move on. Have the wisdom to know you can't change what happened, you can only change how you deal with it. You can be the only one to know what to do with your feelings. You can be sad, remorseful, and angry. Grieve your whole life or say this is the day the Lord hath made. I will rejoice and be glad in it. Don't throw your days away. As you get older you will realize just how precious each one is. Take it from this wrinkled." She pointed to her crow's feet wrinkles on the side of her eye, "and old gray head." She pointed to the top of her head.

This time William got up and threw his arms around her.

"You ain't old. You're just right." They both smiled.

William said, "But at least we won Grammie!"

"Did we win?" William looked puzzled. He at least thought he had this fact correct. "I think of the quote by Joseph Plum Martin, 'I singled out a man and took my aim directly between his shoulders. It was a good mark being a broad-shouldered fellow what became of him I know not. The fire and smoke hid him from my sight. One thing I know that is I took as deliberate aim at him as I ever did of any game in my life but after all I hope I did not kill him although I intended to at the time.' Think about that Willie, he wanted to kill him and prayed he didn't. Do you know when Joseph signed up, he was also fifteen years old?"

William said, "So was Stephen!"

"Just children. War is a horrid game, either play the brutal game to survive but doesn't always mean you won." She straightened back her hair into her bun and readjusted her apron strings. These soldiers can be breaking bread together one day and mortal enemies the next. It can make sons of ministers become murderers and sinners hailed as Saints. So, I don't know. Did we win? We had failed crops, we were broke, members of our family and community dead. If they weren't dead, they would be inflicted with smallpox, injuries, and memories their mind can never erase. Pick your battles wisely and make them worth your every effort. What is the cost of freedom? Freedom can have a heavy price, it's never free."

GENERAL JOHN STARK JULY 31, 1809

"LIVE FREE OR DIE. DEATH IS NOT THE WORST OF EVILS."

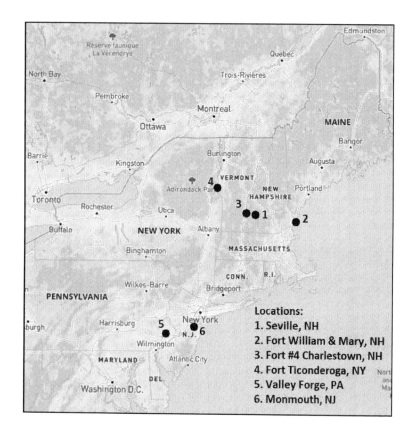

Locations:
1. Seville, NH
2. Fort William & Mary, NH
3. Fort #4 Charlestown, NH
4. Fort Ticonderoga, NY
5. Valley Forge, PA
6. Monmouth, NJ

89

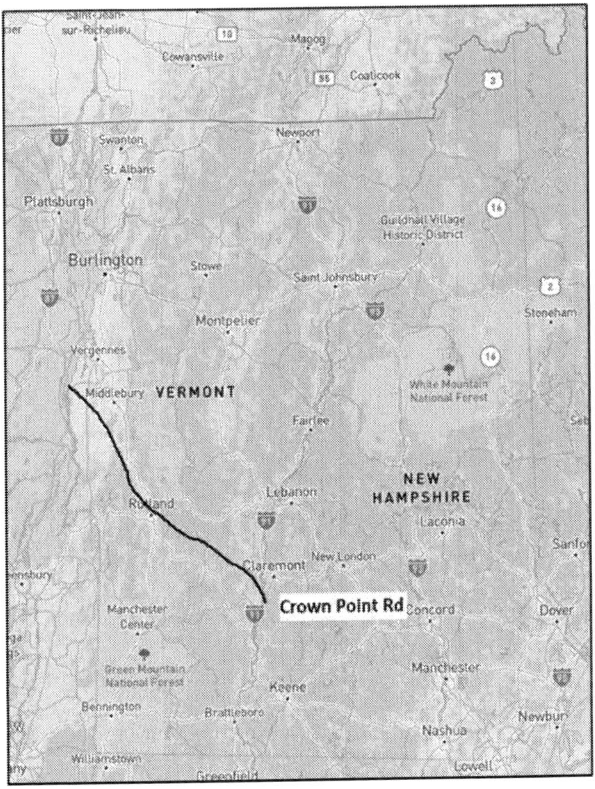
Crown Point Rd
VERMONT
NEW HAMPSHIRE
Burlington
Plattsburgh
Swanton
St. Albans
Newport
Magog
Cowansville
Coaticook
Stowe
Saint Johnsbury
Montpelier
Guildhall Village Historic District
Stoneham
Vergennes
Middlebury
White Mountain National Forest
Fairlee
Lebanon
Rutland
Laconia
Claremont
New London
Concord
Dover
Manchester Center
Green Mountain National Forest
Manchester
Keene
Bennington
Brattleboro
Nashua
Williamstown
Lowell

New Hampshire Warrior is based on Laurel's great, great, great, grandfather's war history during that developing time of our country. She has written: ***My Parents Told Me to NEVER Put Anything into writing, Oops!, The Quest for Quinnie, Hip Hopper the Hip Hop Grasshopper, Miss Olivia goes to Bolivia,*** and ***The Pinboy Chronicles.*** www.lasmithauthor.com

laurelannesmithwrites@gmail.com

Michelle Banning Artist and Art Educator! This is her first published illustrated book. She has been an art educator for 10 years and an artist for many more. She is a mixed media artist who loves clay and crocheting but will play with many other mediums. She loves farming, gardening, and cooking when not creating.

Dwight lives on the banks of the Connecticut River in New Hampshire. He and his wife of 20+ years Heather raised two

beautiful daughters there. When not working at a rock quarry as a foreman and all-around handyman he likes to "wet a line" in any local body of water. He also likes to garden, woodwork, and play in a small band where he sings old country and classic rock.

Like his mother and brother, Cory is a life-long resident of

New Hampshire. He has worked in Federal and State governments for the past 10 years. He is a student of history and will tell you fun facts until it is borderline annoying. He enjoys hiking, fishing, and working on his new home with his lovely wife.

New Hampshire Warrior ~ Live Free or Die

A must have resource for learning and researching the state of New Hampshire during The Revolutionary War.

- **Was Fort William and Mary the first encounter of the Rebellion?**

- **Did you know there was an underwater submarine called The Turtle?**

- **Learn about The Mast Tree Riot, The Spy Ring, and Benedict Arnold.**

"We'll cut the deck. Low card clears the old man's plates."

"Aw, low card again." said William. He had been losing a lot at that game, lately. As William reached to grab the plate, the old man turned and looked right at him, eye to eye.

"Do you boys wanna hear a story?"

William froze. "Sure." William squeaked, his mouth trembling.

George cautiously leaned in to hear the man's words, but to make sure not to get too close.

Old Man Stephen began his tale, "During the war my friends and I would draw cards, just like you boys. But, for us low man would mean being in the front of the line."

George stammered, "Wha, wha, what line?"

"Why the fighting line." Stephen sputtered back, "not something as safe as taking an old man's dishes away."

Follow this journey of historical fiction of the beginnings of our New Hampshire history collaborated with my sons. We researched the military path based on four of our relatives in The Revolutionary War, including my great, great, great, grandfather's during that developing time of our country. He enlisted at age 15 and left his service forever lamed in the arm from the scourge of smallpox. At what price was his freedom?

Made in the USA
Middletown, DE
09 July 2024

56926712R00057